HOW TO BE A GOOD WIFE AND MOTHER

Being The Ideal Wife For An Enviable Life

Dr. Claire Chris

SATISFY EVERY ONE OF THOSE SEXUAL YEARNINGS

UNADULTERATED APPRECIATION, NOT MUCH

FIGURE OUT HOW TO EXPECT YOUR COMPANION'S REQUIREMENTS

DECLARE "YOU'RE RIGHT" — HE'LL LOVE YOU FOR IT

LOVE THE ENTIRETY OF THE MEMBERS OF HIS FAMILY

CONCEDE TO YOUR LIKELY ARRANGEMENTS

CHAPTER THREE

HOW TO MAKE YOUR HUSBAND LOVE YOU

TIP 1. FOCUS ON HAVING A POSITIVE OUTLOOK ON YOURSELF FIRST.

TIP 2. FOCUS ON HOW YOU LOOK.

TIP 3. TRY NOT TO BE SO AVAILABLE.

TIP 4. ACQUIRE BETTER RELATIONSHIP ABILITIES.

TIP 5. CAUSE YOUR SIGNIFICANT OTHER TO HAVE A POSITIVE OUTLOOK ON HIMSELF.

HOW TO HAVE A HAPPY MARRIAGE — TOP TIPS TO IMPROVE YOUR RELATIONSHIP WITH YOUR SPOUSE

TIP 1. WORK ON YOUR SEXUAL COEXISTENCE.

TIP 2. TRY TO CONSTRUCT A VIABLE COMMUNICATION CHANNEL WITH YOUR PARTNER.

TIP 3. AGREE AND TALK ABOUT YOUR FINANCES STRAIGHTFORWARDLY.

TIP 4. GIVE TIME FOR ONE ANOTHER.

CHAPTER FOUR

BEING A GOOD WIFE AND IMPROVING YOUR MARRIAGE

1. PUT FAMILY FIRST

2. BE SUPPORTIVE

3. INVEST QUALITY ENERGY WITH YOUR FAMILY

4. RESOLVE CONFLICTS AMICABLY

5. LOVE UNCONDITIONALLY

HOW TO SUCCEED AS A HUSBAND AND WIFE

HOW TO BE A GOOD WIFE AND MOTHER

1. Be Dedicated
2. Be Compassionate
3. Have the Option To Manage Resources
4. Have the Option To Manage the Home

CHARACTERISTICS OF A GOOD WIFE

1. Be Formally Educated and Stay Educated
2. Be Open-minded
3. You Must Be Domesticated
4. You Must Be Economically Independent
5. You Must Be Managerial and a Budgeter
6. You Must Be Physically Fit
7. You Must Be Sexually Inclined
8. You Must Have Foresight Into the Kind of Home You Want
9. You Should Be Preemptive and Highly Observant
10. Be Hardworking, But Delegate

BEING A GOOD MOTHER – 10 TIPS TO BE THE BEST MOTHER IN THE WORLD

1. Love-based Relationship
2. Be a Decent Teacher
3. Tune in to Your Child – It Makes a Difference
4. You Are the Role Model
5. Invest Energy and Offer
6. Stay Away From What You Need to Keep Away From

INTRODUCTION

There is a famous saying that a decent lady is elusive. This expression is genuine in light of the fact that the characteristics of decent spouse material are not altered by each lady.

The characteristics of decent spouse material include a few perspectives, like what a husband anticipates from a wife, how to be a decent wife and mother, what a husband anticipates from a wife in bed, and what causes a man to revere a lady.

The facts demonstrate that most ladies worry about the question: What do men need in a relationship? Scarcely do any men worry about how to be a decent spouse to a lady who has the characteristics of a decent wife. I feel the subject of how to be a decent spouse is something every man should attempt to worry about, in light of the fact that what wives need from their husbands is similarly pretty much as important as what men pay special mind to in ladies.

Having said that, you should realize that the characteristics of a decent spouse are not something just singles should need to absorb, but rather something reasonable for singles and wedded ladies since it can help you realize how generally a decent wife should be, and improve your marriage, on the off-chance that you are already hitched.

Prior to talking about the characteristics of a decent spouse, I will initially reveal some insights into the things men pay special mind to in ladies.

CHAPTER ONE

What Husbands Expect from Wives in Bed

The room is one of men's number one spots, and they need their spouses to feel a similar way about this spot. Knowing the things, a spouse anticipates from his better half in bed will help you with understanding what your man wants and how you can be best set up to address his issues.

1. Enthusiasm

Men love it when their spouses are amped up for lovemaking. No man needs a lady who is dead cold in bed and doesn't care for making out.

2. Investment

Lovemaking is seriously intriguing when the two players are effectively taking part. Men disdain the possibility of their spouses resting on the bed like a log of wood while they do all the work. They need to see that you are similarly as intrigued by the cycle as they are. They need you to be vivacious, they need to see each one of those moves that you have. So pull out all the stops!

3. Accommodation

It is typical for a man to feel dismissed when his lady isn't surrendering to his cravings and if this proceeds for too long, he may search for another person who can address his issues.

4. Variety

Men like it when their ladies are open to various lovemaking styles and not simply the ordinary missionary style (man on top). They need lovemaking to be intriguing and unconstrained. Not unsurprising and exhausting.

What a Husband Expects From a Wife

There are a few things that spouses want from their wives. They are:

1. Accommodation

Each spouse needs his significant other to be accommodating to him. That way, it is simpler to lead her. No man needs a pompous spouse or one who is scrutinizing his masculinity.

2. Regard

Spouses love it when their wives regard them. It causes them to feel significant and special.

3. Emotions

Emotions are something else men want in their spouses. Men love it when their spouses are heartfelt. It makes marriage fascinating.

4. Uplifting Statements

Men love it when their spouses give them praise. It causes them to feel special and extraordinary. You ought to be your significant other's greatest fan. Acclaim him when he progresses nicely, and figure out how to make light of his deficiencies.

5. Unwaveringness

Unwaveringness implies a ton to men. A man needs to know that he has the help of his significant other on good and bad occasions. This will help him with having a sense of security.

CHAPTER TWO

How to Keep Your Husband Happy

Is it true that you are thinking about how to keep your significant other happy? Do you feel the magic slipping from your marriage and need to return it once more? Is it true that you are searching for approaches to make and keep your significant other happy?

There are numerous seemingly insignificant details and large things you can do to keep your better half happy. Odds are you have both grown a little careless throughout the span of your marriage. Subsequently, you may have allowed a few things to slide and this is causing a rift between you. Nonetheless, it is exceptionally simple to recover that magic with a couple of straightforward advances you can follow to keep your significant other happy.

Hair

Ladies for the most part have long hair and it tends to block the drain inevitably. Rather than allowing it to accumulate and in the end get folded over your significant other's toes, pause for a minute to wipe out the drain each day when you leave the shower. This one straightforward advance can go far to keeping your better half happy.

Comprehend His Work Schedule

Be understanding of when he will return home and the occasions that he needs to burn the midnight oil. Odds are your better half is taking a stab at giving his family a decent living. However, it will start to mess with him and his boss, if you call continually, asking when he will be home. A speedy book or call sometimes is fine. However, don't pester him continually.

Let Him Have His Fun

Clearly, you are the main thing in his life, yet you actually need him to have the option to have his friends as well. Similarly, as you like to go out with your friends, odds are that he might want to spend time with his friends and do guy stuff. Simply ensure that his friends aren't of the hot, female type.

Look After Yourself

While you don't need to maintain a specific weight or hair tone, don't allow yourself absolutely to let go, when you have been together for some time. A person actually loves somebody who invests heavily in their appearance, so make certain to keep yourself looking decent. While this doesn't imply that you need to clean up to perfection constantly, putting on a little makeup will go far.

Try Not to Hide the Bills

If you have gone through a lot of cash, be forthright and legitimate about it. It may not be the most lovely discussion, yet he would prefer to catch wind of it from you, rather than get an unexpected call from a lender.

Plan a Date Night

Make certain to incorporate accomplishing something that will satisfy him. For example, going to see the most recent action movie or go to a restaurant that you both appreciate. Make certain to act as you did when you initially began dating, and focus on one another throughout the evening.

Try Not to Go to Bed Mad at Each Other

A spouse who is happy is normally very much refreshed. Notwithstanding, this rest will not come should you hit the sack irate with one another. Make certain to settle any issues prior to hitting the hay.

How to Keep Your Husband Satisfied Emotionally

Being explicitly in tune with your better half isn't the solitary thing that you ought to be stressed over in your relationship. Having extraordinary sex isn't anything, contrasted with being genuinely one with him. Indeed, these two perspectives are not at all similar. So how might you function at keeping your hubby sincerely fulfilled?

See Through His Eyes

Perceive what you look like through his eyes. Envision how he would depict your relationship as a team. Don't simply continue to consider you, or what you need – doing so will be out of line for him. This man has the right to be content, as well, remember that.

Satisfy Every One of Those Sexual Yearnings

Also, this is for both of you! Don't simply continue to give him what he needs when afterward, you are still left needing. Fulfill his sexual dreams and disclose to him how he could likewise fulfill yours.

Unadulterated Appreciation, Not Much

Continuously be thankful for every one of the things that your significant other contributes in your relationship. A person who realizes that he's being valued will work more diligently at giving you more. He'll likewise feel much manlier – and that is unquestionably something that you would need him to feel!

Figure Out How to Expect Your Companion's Requirements

Show to your better half that you're willing to share his obligations, regardless of whether you'll need him to play his part by cutting the grass on occasion. One of his requirements is to be free from time to time, so release him during such minutes. Know everything that he needs and offer it all to him. However long it isn't hurting your relationship, spoil your better half with these things.

Declare "You're Right" – He'll Love You for It

If you need to accentuate what you need, make your statement clear. Absolutely never belittle your man by causing him to feel that he's substandard. You can downplay the fights, if you figure out how to state your needs and wants in a quiet way.

Love the Entirety of the Members of His Family

In spite of the fact that some of them may not be that adorable, still, you need to make every effort to cherish his family. They are the ones he grew up with, so figure out how to accept them into your life.

Concede to Your Likely Arrangements

All things considered, you're a couple, so it is pointless to plan for two separate fates. You need to concur or you'll always be unable to form a serviceable arrangement for your family.

CHAPTER THREE

How to Make Your Husband Love You

We become hopelessly enamored when we get hitched, needing the romance to keep going forever. In any case, before you come to terms with the fact that there's work to be done, you need to figure out how to make your significant other love you. So here are five tips to help you re-touch the romance in your marriage…

Tip 1. Focus on having a positive outlook on yourself first.

Emotions are infectious. So how you feel can, without much of a stretch, make a change in your better half's feelings. If you need your better half to have more affection for you, start by having more affection for yourself. Rather than demanding that your significant other change, change yourself first.

Tip 2. Focus on how you look.

Do you like the way you look right now? Don't simply spruce up to go out. Focus on what you look like at home also. Work towards looking and feeling more like that pleasant person your significant other became hopelessly enamored with. After marriage, it's not difficult to fall into the groove of not thinking often about your appearance anymore. Despite the fact that your significant other says looks don't make any difference, he will never oppose you looking hot.

Tip 3. Try not to be so available.

Men need space. To give your better half his space, focus on doing things that exclude him. You can:

- Converse with different companions
- Read a book
- Invest energy with the children
- … and so forth

To guarantee romance in your relationship, attempt to be a little more enigmatic. The less attention he has from you, the more he'll need to converse with you to discover what you're doing.

Tip 4. Acquire better relationship abilities.

We as a whole see things in an unexpected way. Thus, you may feel your significant other doesn't cherish you since you don't understand his point of view. Figure out how to take a look at affection diversely and you may understand he adores you more than you used to think. Examine your assumptions regarding romance and marriage with your better half, and you might be astounded at what you find out about your significant other.

Tip 5. Cause your significant other to have a positive outlook on himself.

Cause your significant other to feel like he's your number one, regardless. Think about this: we as a whole prefer to invest energy in people who cause us to have a positive outlook on ourselves. If you're ready to discover and concentrate on what is acceptable about your companion, he will feel your appreciation in one way or another and shift his affections towards you. Take a look at him with appreciation in your eyes and he will not be able to avoid falling head over heels for you once more.

How to Have a Happy Marriage – Top Tips to Improve Your Relationship With Your Spouse

Having a happy marriage is to be sure something that most couples wish for after the wedding obviously, but when marriage is tested with added needs like children, a new home, accounts and bills, keeping the fire burning in the relationship may require a little work. Figuring out how to have a happy marriage not just in the initial months, but all through your lifetime can for sure be a test.

Regardless of whether you are somebody who just got hitched or somebody well into a falling apart marriage, here are a couple of tips that may help you construct a happy marriage and keep away from separating, and keep up or bring back the spark in your relationship.

Tip 1. Work on your sexual coexistence.

A satisfying sexual coexistence is for sure a significant component of a happy marriage. If your sexual coexistence has been something that has gotten a daily schedule, you might need to discover new approaches to make your lovemaking. Obviously, a little examination will help you track down 101 different ways to learn the most proficient methods for satisfying your partner in bed. Find out about the desires people have in lovemaking. Assuming you are not a person who is into a "sexless marriage," you should bring back the desire and the allure that you once had. Conversation plays a significant part in this specific issue.

Obviously, having the option to communicate transparently to your partner your sexual requirements will help a ton, yet recall too that this isn't just about "your needs." You likewise need to think about your partner's needs too.

Tip 2. Try to construct a viable communication channel with your partner.

A disintegrating marriage is frequently an aftereffect of being not able to discuss well with your partner, or choosing to do so in a way that isn't effective. Absence of productive communication can without a doubt place your marriage in stress, yet practice can be a good starting point in aiding you on the best way to have a happy marriage. Listening is quite possibly the most overlooked ability that is vital in building sound and open communication with your partner. Figure out how to listen more and you will discover more noteworthy changes on how you communicate.

Tip 3. Agree and talk about your finances straightforwardly.

Monetary issues and clashes are likewise among the things that can cause clashes in your marriage and as long as you are open in discussing your finances, particularly when you are living on a budget, you can likewise make it simpler to deal with how to have a happy marriage.

Tip 4. Give time for one another.

In spite of the fact that needs may increment in a marriage, it is important not to neglect making quality time for your partner. It is important not to take one another for granted. One of the normal mix-ups of wedded people is underestimating their partners, as they frequently imagine that living under one roof is sufficient for them, or sitting together at supper is sufficient. To work at a happy marriage, you need to ensure that you have a decent laugh together on occasions. You get to know one another, just you two together, or in any event, supporting each other particularly when one needs it badly.

CHAPTER FOUR

Being a good Wife and Improving Your Marriage

To be a decent spouse to your significant other and have a fruitful marriage, you should figure out how to do the following:

1. Put Family First

Your family should consistently come first when you are settling on your choices. This is one of the characteristics of a decent spouse.

2. Be Supportive

Your better half will require your help now and again. Be willing and prepared to give it with his goals, so that he remains charmed by you and your home continues moving along as expected.

3. Invest Quality Energy With Your Family

Your better half requires your full focus. Make quality time every day for both of you to remain close, outwardly and inwardly.

4. Resolve Conflicts Amicably

Clashes are inevitable in each marriage. In any case, the manner in which they are settled can either fortify or obliterate a relationship. So you should put forth sincere attempts to see how your companion responds when angry, and work out a way to best respond to him so things don't get muddled between both of you.

5. Love Unconditionally

You should cherish and uphold your better half in the good and bad moments. This way he will realize that you have his back and will confide in you absolutely and feel more charmed by you.

Marriage Takes Commitment, Love and Affection

Everyone knows the phrase "Love is blind." My understanding of this means being centered around what you are going to try to make essential in marriage.

Marriage isn't for the weak-willed, indeed one should invest in a life of companionship. Any time a person chooses to wed somebody, they are imparting to the world that they have discovered what they have been searching for as long as they can remember.

Can we truly say we truly know the person we've wedded? A deep question to pose, anyway it's one worth talking about. Trust your own instincts to reveal to you whether you truly know the person you wedded.

Now and again, with the person you wedded, you may feel like you know them and at different occasions it's like living with an outsider. For what reason is this so?

A profound question, and I will answer it for you. Simply, people change and at times it's unnoticeable and on others it's recognizable. Regardless of whether you will notice the changes, development is always happening.

Love assumes an essential part of marriage – or it ought to. If you are talking with your partner and you inquire as to whether they love you and they say, "You have no clue about how I feel about you," it very well might be the ideal opportunity for additional conversation.

Making a full and complete obligation to marriage is important, on the grounds that you would prefer not to live with somebody you dislike. Love rises above errors, miscommunication and deficiencies, ones that we as a whole will experience throughout everyday life. Unequivocal love implies we will contribute somewhat a greater amount of our own selves while we decipher and comprehend the things about our companions we disagree with.

Marriage takes responsibility, love and friendship, and it's dependent upon us to work with what we have, as a feature of marriage. Love assumes a critical part in marriage, in that it's a reward within a marriage, since you can be companions with your life partner and back them, regardless of whether you disagree with their choices on issues influencing you and your children.

More or less, go into marriage with your eyes totally open. Work on turning into the best life partner you can be, and keep on making great experiences for you and your family. Responsibility, love and warmth will give significant advantages to your marriage and it's dependent upon you to make your marriage succeed.

How to Succeed as a Husband and Wife

Prevailing as a couple requires commitment towards making your marriage work. Working as a couple implies that you both need to cooperate to address normal marriage predicaments and to function collectively to keep the marriage solid.

The path to an effective marriage is communication. I am aware of people who are hitched yet they don't sleep in the same bed – the two of them have their different rooms. You don't need this to occur, and the most ideal approach to forestall this is with good communication.

Communication is the thing that is needed for a couple. If you can provide great communication, you have a decent possibility of having your marriage keep going for a long time. You would prefer not to be a couple that looks great outwardly while privately, things aren't as great as they appear – so remember this.

To prevail as a couple, great communication is vital. If there are any conflicts between you, make certain to work it out so you can resolve any issues that exist between you. Your marriage can be made effective – however, it requires both of you being in total agreement as far as conversing with one another.

Something else that you need to do as a couple is to go out on dates. In effective relationships, you will find that people often have nights out where they go out and have fun with one another. I as of now go out on dates all the time with my lady, and it has proven to be what holds our relationship together.

Do you and your companion take a seat at the table and have supper together? If you do not, you ought to. If you have children, eating at the kitchen table and having the entire family there is a decent method of improving the nuclear family. Bonds will be made and you will also get acquainted by eating together. I am aware of families who don't eat at the table together and due to this, they're not as close they ought to be.

You don't need to allow this to happen to you. Make it a highlight to sit down with your family and have important discussions. As a couple, this is important. Not exclusively will this reinforce your family, but it will fortify your marriage too – so remember this.

As a couple, you must be focused on each other and make sacrifices to make your marriage work. There are a wide range of things that you can do to improve your marriage, and the tips in this book are only a few of them. Make certain to remember these tips at whatever point you feel the gloss of your marriage disappearing.

Use these tips to have the sort of marriage that you wish for.

How to Be a Good Wife and Mother

To be the sort of spouse that makes her significant other happy and her children happy, you ought to figure out how to do the following.

1. Be Dedicated

Men don't care for it when their spouses rely upon them for everything. You ought to have an unmistakable overflow of energy. Get going, accomplish something you love, and he will esteem and regard you more – but not just him, your children will as well.

2. Be Compassionate

You ought to have the option to identify with the feelings of your family, companions, and everybody around you – if not, they will feel detached from you.

3. Have the Option To Manage Resources

To be a decent spouse and mother, you should have the option to oversee resources carefully, so your family doesn't run out of them.

4. Have the Option To Manage the Home

Your partner won't generally be with the children. He needs to know that he can rely upon you to deal with the undertakings of the home well, with or without his input.

Characteristics of a Good Wife

Coming up next are the characteristics a lady should have to qualify as great spouse material.

1. Be Formally Educated and Stay Educated

Being well educated distinguishes you and accords respect from your partner. It helps and adjusts your thinking. It improves your character. It opens up the world to you with captivating freedoms to discover.

Move with the world. Be up to date with current events in your nearby and expanded circles. Get more degrees and accreditations, while you seek after a vocation.

2. Be Open-minded

Being open-minded is your capacity to handle information without being affected. You can channel each event and experience every circumstance without permitting distractions from your companion, friends, and the general public.

When you have done this, you can give yourself the space to think independently in your opinions of your life partner's opinions, and see when they are sensible. This is the place where bargaining comes into a marriage. Being a lady doesn't make you powerless – neither does being a spouse cause you to lose your independence and individuality.

Being open-minded brings confidence; it guarantees to your significant other that you can't be controlled. A huge number of ladies are exposed to troubles, since they have been conditioned to believe that they have no life separated from the existence of their spouses.

They are inert. They can't have an independent perspective. They can't stand up or air an opinion. They can't make strides. Love is excellent, however when it enslaves your capacity to think, at that point you are in never-ending subjugation.

3. You Must Be Domesticated

Being house-proud means knowing about how a house runs, running it, and keeping up the interactions. The cycle of morning, afternoon, and evening concerning the running of a house is vital.

You eat, you shower, you cook, you rest, you entertain, you oblige guests, you clean, you cook, you care for the home, you organize and adjust, you care for your children and spouse – the work continues forever. This requires your insight into how to make it all work.

4. You Must Be Economically Independent

You should have your money separate from your spouse's. Two purposes behind this are: each person is physiologically determined by their own needs, which must be entirely fulfilled without help from anyone else. Furthermore, there must be a backup account in case your better half loses his job, or passes away. That account is your financial independence. It additionally gives you a feeling of significance and fulfillment.

5. You Must Be Managerial and a Budgeter

This is your capacity to handle the current circumstances promptly and to plan for current needs versus future circumstances, concerning available money. That is, saving money for present and future requirements.

Planning is the ability to keep accessible money ready for any given time frame. It goes with being organized. A budgeter controls foolish spending. Most men can't deal with their cash. They go through it as soon as cash comes in. You should come in now by helping him with overseeing it.

6. You Must Be Physically Fit

Your body should not be a burden to you, except in times of illness. Fitness should be imbued in your persona. Exercise, eat quality food, see friends – those snapshots of laughing with friends are restorative. Rest, and take naps when essential.

7. You Must Be Sexually Inclined

One of the center main thrusts of every marriage is sex. You should anticipate it. Initiate it. Make your better half anticipate it. Stay clean consistently, dress fittingly and enticingly in the house, but be wary if there are children and guests in the house. Be that as it may, if they are not in the house, throw caution to the wind. Sending the right vibe is appealing to your significant other. It isn't about sex alone, however, it likewise includes intimacy, and time for private talks.

8. You Must Have Foresight Into the Kind of Home You Want

It is regularly said that a lady rules the home. You should have a psychological image of the home you need and work towards it. Fight with anything or anybody stopping you from having your perfect home. If you don't have an image of your fantasy home, life will become an unremarkable one for you, and you will have nothing to anticipate in your home.

9. You Should Be Preemptive and Highly Observant

Being preemptive is having the option to understand what somebody will do or say before they do it or say it. This is possible by you being attentive. We are creatures of habit. Being perceptive will uncover a person's behaviors to you and you will know when the habits change. You ought to have the option to foresee your significant other's mindset on most occasions. Moreover, your children's. Emotional episodes are results of our reactions to our current circumstances. Thus, plans are dependent upon natural changes. Along these lines, when there is a change in the climate – I don't mean the actual climate, but the monetary, romantic, and so forth – you ought to have the option to seize the opportunity to change.

10. Be Hardworking, But Delegate

This is quite possibly the main characteristic of a decent spouse. Lethargy lets down even the easiest of things. Be up and doing things – however, don't stress yourself with work. Do what should be done at the right time. You can't do everything, you may make yourself sick. Allocate jobs to your children. Whatever your better half needs to deal with, advise him, and remind him if it isn't finished. If you have help in the house, great!

Being a Good Mother – 10 Tips to Be the Best Mother

Capable nurturing and providing a loving home are conceivable with the help of a mother. Living in a challenging situation, moms have many challenges. I'm certain each mother needs their best efforts to make a decent parent. Here are ten hints that will help with getting down to business and return to being loving, and turning into a decent mother.

1. Love-based Relationship

A family is comprised of love bonds. It is a link between all relatives, and the mother holds an essential obligation to show love. This helps children become well balanced and makes everyone want to get along. Love helps with leading and shaping great relationships.

2. Be a Decent Teacher

Learning through a mother at home turns into a solid foundation for a child and it helps them with confronting difficulties and becoming capable later on. Every child is different, and a teacher needs to adjust their methodology of instructing, ensuring that the child learns and gets it. Try not to be too stern a teacher; this might influence the learning stages.

3. Tune in to Your Child – It Makes a Difference

Children anticipate that their mother or father should hear them out when they talk. As moms invest more energy bringing up children, tuning in to them mindfully and recognizing them helps them to stay connected. It additionally helps with understanding their skills and knowledge.

4. You Are the Role Model

At the point when a mother is a teacher, it is vital for her to be a role model for her child. Keep in mind, whatever the child notices, and learns through a mother, will show in them as they develop. Consequently, observe every one of your actions and words. Always be polite and respectful.

5. Invest Energy and Offer

For a functioning woman, it is hard to have her own time. Have a timetable and be accessible to invest energy with the children. Sit with them, play and talk. Despite the fact that you may have less time, it turns into a daily practice and helps them with growing up. Needless to say, moms at home have constant time with the children, so use it.

6. Stay Away From What You Need to Keep Away From

Living standards differ from one home to another. Avoid having children being presented with specific practices at home that you believe aren't right. Fend them off and never give any opportunity for them to become ingrained and cause problems later.

7. Help and Guide Your Child

Be a positive mother, and guide your child when required. If the child experiences an issue, help them with understanding what made the issue, and how to avoid it later on. Give alternative arrangements and help them with getting past it. Intervene when required and mentor them.

8. Keep up Discipline at Home

Rules made by moms at home should rigorously followed by their children. Get them adjusted to this, and it will be simpler to follow. Declare disciplinary actions whenever needed, and tell them that your words can't be underestimated.

9. Persuade and Appreciate

Move and motivate your child in the most ideal ways possible. If you discover them being great at something, appreciate it. Work with them to improve their abilities and teach them to learn more.

10. Way of Life and Family Esteem

Building a home resembles building a realm. Customs and living standards come to children through their parents. The mother assumes a significant part in teaching their children to understand their way of life and the upsides of their families, which will help them with adapting to the world.

Giving consideration and care to a child is the most important part in an upbringing. Great moms prevail by giving time, showing love, and addressing all the issues of a child. Nurturing is a repeated interaction and a few repeated examples will affect them over time. Be that as it may, a person's experience, age, foundation and schooling adds to being a decent mother.

CHAPTER FIVE

How to Make Your Marriage Successful.

A successful marriage requires a great deal of persistence and work to make it happen. At the point when two people live under the same roof there will undoubtedly be problems and issues. However, it isn't hard to keep a happy and amicable connection between the two of you. Here are a few activities to keep a decent, effective and durable connection between couples.

Be Realistic

Many couples go into marriage with ridiculous assumptions. Life isn't a walk in the park, as a large portion of us envision. Have a solid understanding of what to anticipate and what not to anticipate from your marriage. Talk with your fiancé ahead of time to know and share your assumptions about the marriage so that there will not be any false impressions to discover later. The more open you are, the more joyful you will be in your marriage.

Show Love and Appreciation

Life can be challenging on occasions. However, when you have the adoration and backing of your partner, it turns out to be all the more simple to confront even the hardest circumstances. Never let your partner feel disliked or unappreciated. Try not to hold back with your adoration, warmth and actual touch for your partner. However, busy you are, you can figure out an ideal opportunity for a quick kiss, an embrace or a quick call to your loved one. The more you attempt to cause your partner to feel significant and special, the more happy you will be.

Give Attention to Your Spouse

Often, couples underestimate each other, which can damage a relationship. Try not to continue to bother your partner to do things the way in which you need to. There is a maxim: "Give attention and get attention." If you need your companion or children to show regard to you, it is important that you show regard as well. Be aware of your partner and his feelings and you will get the regard you deserve.

Resolve Fights and Arguments Quick

One of the significant reasons that couples break up is leaving fights unresolved. It is very common that a couple may have a lack of interest – however, resolve the situation right away. Try not to stop for a second to say sorry, should you have committed an error, and offer peace so it will not occur again. Try not to bring up old issues that have been settled when you are having a fight.

Great Communication

Good communication is the way to a happy marriage. Never let marital weariness creep into your relationship. Talk with one another as much as you can, and acquire a superior comprehension of one another. This way you can keep away from false impressions. It would be a good idea to dedicate one day a week to you two. Spending holidays together at least once a year will also be a great way to improve your communication levels.

Be Faithful to Your Spouse

There can be temptations. However, should you regard the promise you made to your companion by remaining faithful and not betray his trust, you are probably going to be compensated by his devotion and trust as well. This is perhaps the most fundamental feature to make a marriage work.

Make Compromises

You can't get all that you need. You need to make a few trade offs sooner or later in life for your partner to make your relationship work.

Plan Surprises

Plan surprises for your partner and it will cause them to feel happy and special. Always remember a special day for you or your partner, as it offers you a chance to celebrate together.

Openness and Honesty

Maintain openness and honesty in whatever you do. Never keep secrets or lie to your partner. It is alright to have friends of the opposite sex, yet ensure that your life partner knows about them. Acquaint your partner with them or better still, meet them in the company of your partner. This can strengthen the trust factor in your relationship.

Remembering the above ideas and practicing them in your marriage can make it an enduring and effective one.

CHAPTER SIX

How to Keep Your Happy Marriage Through All Life's Struggles

Life is once in a while awesome, yet there are always going to be fights and problems which can put an enormous burden on a marriage. There are step by step instructions to keep a happy marriage, regardless of those things which appear to be a problem for any couple. Yet the reward of decreasing arguments and promoting romance and bliss really make overcoming challenges simpler and will diminish any problems in a nearly karmic way.

There is no mysterious equation to keeping a marriage happy. However, there are a ton of little things you ought to accomplish that will work, regardless of what kind of marriage you have. This includes: professional couples, married with kids, marriage with pets, young, old and everything in between! Some ideas that will help you reach better outcomes are:

Obligation to Marital Happiness

Above all else, bliss isn't something that mystically arrives in your lap. Happiness doesn't come solely from your financial success, nor is it from achievements, children or many other things that people regularly expect it to come from. Bliss is a decision, through bad and good times, that you should focus on supporting so it turns into an inevitable outcome.

This doesn't involve huge efforts or a ton of additional time. However, it requires a steady attention to what you are doing and adding to your relationship to make your existence with your life partner and children better and more joyful consistently. Nobody else can do this. It is dependent upon you above all else, and this interest in bliss will be irresistible to your whole family.

Focus on the Good Rather Than the Bad

One issue numerous people face when circumstances become difficult, and sometimes when everything in life appears to be good, is to focus on the negative. At the point when life appears to be extraordinary, this might be on the grounds that you have become fixated on eliminating anything marginally bad about it. And when things are down, it turns out to be a lot simpler to see many negative things.

When you disregard the bad things, for example, towels left on the floor, an occasional bowl or cup left unwashed, badly folded clothes in the drawers or 100 other small habits, rather focus on what you love about your life partner.

Remind yourself and focus on those things that you adore. The manner in which they hold you when you are sad, their enormous laugh, the way they cook your favorite food at the weekend, how magnificently they play with the children, or whatever makes you feel great inside.

Show Appreciation More Often

At the point when life gets hard or distracting, if we are complacent in a marriage we tend to neglect praising our partners on their activities, since we have become accustomed to them. Indeed, it can often be the case that you get accustomed to all the beneficial things your partner does that you consider them to be ordinary, and begin needing more effort and more special things to make you happy.

This can be toxic and a straightforward solution for such things is to make sure to praise your partner frequently and show genuine appreciation for even the littlest of things. If they tidy something up without you asking, when you for the most part manage that thing, make a point of saying thank you. If they burn through some additional energy to get dressed up when going out, say they look extraordinary. Whenever they are simply tackling their work but show something extra like picking the kids up from school, make sure to incidentally say thanks to them for doing this.

If you are sincere about this, it is simple, fast and doesn't just cause your partner to feel more appreciated and cherished, it builds communication and you will find that they really want to show you appreciation back. Furthermore, a relationship where praise has been omitted from your communication will find that there is no communication either way, as neither spouse nor wife offers anything, and neither gets it back in return. This makes for an unhappy marriage and frequently causes anger and resentment, and a slide into focusing on the negatives.

Show Respect to Your Spouse

As has been mentioned, we will in general underestimate our spouse in all that they do. Familiarity breeds contempt, as the idiom goes, yet it doesn't need to if that we decide to be aware of how we act.

If you have at any point discovered yourself directing feelings toward your partner that you could never say to your friends or your colleagues, since it might offend them, then you might be sliding down a negative path. It could be on the grounds that you think they love you and something disrespectful won't be minded, or that you are so agreeable in your communication with your partner that you feel being to-the-point and showing your actual feelings of anger will get to the issue quicker; this is certifiably not a decent method to communicate regardless of whether it appears to be proficient.

Your life partner is a person like any other and showing irreverence to them harms them and damages your relationship. If you choose to be decent or to be correct and to bring up it an issue, then what do you think will create joy? Be decent, and communicating your concerns should be possible.

Try Not to Nitpick

Just as you should focus on the great aspects of your partner and disregard the little things, you ought to likewise work this into how you communicate. Picking your fights can be a significant aspect of how you approach marital issues, in light of the fact that there will always be some disagreements, regardless of how compatible you both are.

At whatever point there is an issue you want to raise, ask as to whether this is truly worth starting a fight about. Is it truly significant enough to make more grief, or should you let this one slide? While you feel all issues should be settled, if you are continually irritated about one thing or another your partner will also begin to sift through the things you are saying, given that most issues are usually minor. If you don't criticize when you do raise a concern, they will give undeniably more consideration to you too, so save your critical thinking discussions for those things that do matter.

Similarly, if you are open-minded toward the little things, you will discover your partner will show tolerance for any of your bad habits, and life will be more joyful – if perhaps somewhat more chaotic. Which would you like?

More Touching and Intimacy

New lovebirds often can't let go of each other, as each second they need to be close and personal. Embracing, contacting, kissing and touching all form closeness and affection, which can drop off over the course of a long relationship.

Moms particularly discover themselves all loved out from having children, and have minimal energy left to provide for their spouses, which can build little feelings of resentment after some time. These can be a hindrance to conjugal bliss.

You don't have to return to the exciting days of your wedding trip, yet ensuring you occasionally hold your partner for more than a quick embrace will work wonders. Hold them and tell them you like their closeness at that point, and ensure that you increase your physical contact. Add a couple of more kisses, hold their shoulders with a loving embrace when they are accomplishing something, and perform other little activities to do much more to show love than any words.

Set Aside a Few Minutes for Just You Two

Work, children and a busy life can now and again make private time between you two hard. When it does happen, private discussions are about work, children and your schedules, also making it less of a private encounter!

Not that you need to remove these things from your conversations totally. However, making the effort to be apart from everyone else and together without the children asking for your time or attention, or having your phone going off at regular intervals, is fundamental for reconnecting to one another.

There doesn't have to be a need to spend a long time together – simply an evening here or day every few weeks, or even thirty minutes after the children are sleeping, to share some time together in discussion over a drink. This is critical to help remind you both that you are living with somebody who you love and loves you back, and that you are not simply a mother or father, and that you are something beyond workers and providers. Remind yourselves you are two people, in love and married, and satisfy the fantasies about being happy over all obstacles.

CHAPTER SEVEN

Conclusion

Thank you for reading this book. By now you should realize that there is no restriction to the ways that you can work out how to be that wife your better half requires. So keep your mind open always to inventive ways you can remain close to your partner.